FLIPPIN' good

You might be celebrating a major milestone or simply the weekend, at home with a few close friends or in a parking lot with a crowd of strangers, but be assured...

LITTLE MOMENTS OF HAPPINESS START AT THE GRILL.

ISBN-13: 978-1-56383-536-0
Item #7139

**Printed in the USA
by G&R Publishing Co.**

Distributed By:

507 Industrial Street
Waverly, IA 50677

www.cqbookstore.com

gifts@cqbookstore.com

 CQ Products

 CQ Products

 @cqproducts

 @cqproducts

TAKING IT ON THE ROAD?

Before you leave home:

- Make sure you have a grill and propane or charcoal. And plenty of it.

- Pack a grill brush, tongs, spatula, meat thermometer, and a timer.

- Do your food prep – like marinating and seasoning – ahead of time so it's ready to hit the grates when you arrive.

- Don't forget side dishes and snacks.

- Pack raw meat separately in your cooler to prevent contact with other foods.

- Have enough ice along to keep foods from spoiling.

- Stock plenty of soap, water, and disposable towels for the day.

At your destination:

- Set your grill a reasonable distance away from your vehicle so you don't damage your paint or ignite the gas tank.

- Use a meat thermometer when grilling meat, and make sure you're grilling in a well-lit area so you can actually see the thermometer!

- Fully extinguish the hot coals of a charcoal grill before placing it back in your car. Enough said.

Above all else, grill carefully – it's all fun & games until somebody burns their buns!

These loaded salmon patties take only a few minutes to cook, so you can have dinner ready and on the picnic table in no time at all. And who doesn't love a flippin' fast meal?!

GRILL PAN SALMON PATTIES

1 (14.75 oz.) can salmon, drained & flaked

2 finely chopped green onions

½ C. finely diced red bell pepper

2 T. chopped fresh parsley

1 lightly beaten egg

2 T. lemon juice

¼ C. panko bread crumbs

Sea salt & coarse black pepper to taste

Guacamole

Mix the salmon, green onions, bell pepper, parsley, egg, lemon juice, bread crumbs, salt, and black pepper. Form into eight to ten *(½" thick)* firm patties; freeze for 15 minutes or chill for ½ hour.

Set a grill pan on the grill and preheat on medium or medium-high heat. Coat the pan heavily with cooking spray.

Add the chilled patties. Hear 'em sizzle? Yeah, that's a good thing. Heat about 5 minutes on each side, flipping carefully when grill marks appear and the patties hold their shape. Top with some guacamole. *Delectable!*

Perfect Beer Pairings

With salmon or chicken? **Try a Pilsner.**

Spicy food? **Go with an IPA.**

Smoky flavors? **Get out the Amber Ale.**

Burgers? Bacon? Chocolate? **Porter's the way to go.**

One beer to go with just about everything? **Lager.**

Makes 8

Layers of flavor all rolled up together to create a hot dog you can really sink your canines into!

ROLL OVER BIG DOGS

Olive oil

3 poblano peppers

2 to 3 T. of your favorite mustard *(we used whole grain)*

1 to 2 T. chopped onion

1 to 2 T. salsa

Black pepper to taste

1 (16 oz.) can refried beans *(any variety)*

16 (8") flour tortillas

1 (16 oz.) pkg. shredded Colby Jack cheese

8 (¼ lb.) hot dogs

Cheese dip, sour cream & salsa

Grease the grill grate and preheat the grill on high heat.

Drizzle oil over the peppers and set them on the hot grill, cooking until they're nicely charred, turning occasionally. Remove and discard the skin, leaving some of the char in place; coarsely chop the peppers, discarding seeds.

Mix the mustard, onion, salsa, black pepper, and beans together and spread evenly over one side of each tortilla. Divide the cheese and chopped peppers over the beans on half the tortillas and stack those on top of the remaining ones, bean sides up; set aside.

Heat the hot dogs on the grill until they're cooked the way you like 'em. Remove 'em from the grill but don't turn off the heat. Place a grilled dog on each of the tortilla stacks and roll up to enclose that puppy tightly inside. Spritz the roll-ups with cooking spray and set them on the grill until they have nice grill marks all around, turning as needed.

Set out cheese dip, sour cream, and salsa for dipping.

Spiral Fun Dogs

Push a long skewer through the length of a hot dog. Starting at one end of the dog, use a sharp knife to make a diagonal cut until your knife rests on the skewer. Make one long continuous spiral cut all around the hot dog through the other end, turning the dog as you go. Remove the skewer and grill the dog. Place in a bun and fill the nooks & crannies with condiments! A fun new trick for your dog!

Makes about 7 cups

Sweet corn tastes its absolute best when you buy it fresh in season, but in a pinch, you could substitute frozen ears for this recipe.

CHARRED CORN SALAD

Remove the husks and silk from 6 ears of sweet corn. Brush the corn lightly with vegetable oil. Grill over medium heat until tender and lightly charred, turning occasionally. Set aside until just cool enough to handle.

Cut the kernels off the cobs and put the corn into a bowl. Core, seed, and dice a green bell pepper, ½ of a small red onion, and a couple of juicy Roma tomatoes and toss them in there, too *(you can also char the bell pepper before dicing it, if you'd like)*; add a handful of chopped fresh cilantro, a big drizzle of olive oil, and a squeeze of fresh lime juice. Season liberally with salt and black pepper and stir to combine. Chill at least 30 minutes for flavors to blend, and you'll be rewarded with crisp and smoky lusciousness!

Servings vary

This dessert idea is super-fast, crazy-easy, and just plain delicious! Made on a grill pan to preserve every last drop of goodness.

BOOZY BANANA BOATS

Set a grill pan on the grill and preheat on high heat. For each banana, whisk together 1½ tsp. honey, 1½ tsp. rum, and a sprinkle of cinnamon. Cut unpeeled bananas lengthwise through the stem ends, following the curve of the fruit. Coat the grill pan and the cut side of each banana with cooking spray; set bananas on the hot pan, cut side down. Grill for a couple of minutes, until nice grill marks appear.

Flip them over and brush liberally with the honey-rum mixture before taking them off the grill. Spray on some whipping cream and dig in. *Heck yes!*

Serves 4

There's a lot of flavor and a ton of texture packed into these turkey burgers! Give 'em a try – we promise you'll gobble 'em up.

SANTE FE BURGERS

- 1 lb. ground turkey
- 1 C. shredded Mexican cheese blend
- ¼ C. salsa, plus more for serving
- ¼ C. crushed tortilla chips
- ¼ C. thinly sliced green onion
- 1 tsp. smoked chili powder
- ½ tsp. garlic salt
- Melted butter
- 8 Kaiser rolls
- Tomato, lettuce & red onion

Grease the grill grate and preheat the grill on medium-high heat.

Toss the ground turkey, cheese, ¼ cup salsa, tortilla chips, green onion, chili powder, and garlic salt in a bowl and mix together lightly. Shape into four ¾"-thick patties and press a dimple into the center.

Grill until the internal temperature of the meat reaches 160°, turning to brown both sides. During the last minute or two, spread butter over the cut sides of the rolls and grill until lightly toasted.

Serve burgers on the toasted rolls with salsa, tomato, lettuce, and red onion.

For the Best Burgers

- *Make all patties the same size, guaranteeing they cook at the same rate.*

- *Don't man-handle your patties, lest you end up with tough burgers.*

- *Press a dimple into the center of each patty to help maintain their shape.*

- *Season liberally when your patties are ready to hit the grill. Salting too soon could dry out the meat. Bummer.*

- *Check the temp with an instant-read thermometer; don't poke too often, though, or all that wonderful juice will escape.*

- *Choose hefty buns to stand up to big, juicy burgers. Smaller, thinner patties can handle a softer bun.*

Turn your outdoor party into a fiesta with these zesty grilled options. Guaranteed to flip your sombrero!

GRILLED TACO SPREAD

Ooo's & Ahh's Fish Tacos: Mix 6 T. tequila, 2 T. vegetable oil, ¼ C. lime juice, 4 tsp. lime zest, a 2" piece of fresh ginger *(peeled & minced)*, 2 tsp. minced garlic, 2 tsp. each salt and sugar, 1 tsp. ground cumin, and ½ tsp. each cinnamon and black pepper; add 2 lbs. tilapia fillets, flip to coat, and chill 1 hour. Grill the fillets on greased foil over low heat, until the fish flakes easily. *Serves 8*

Run-for-the-Border Chicken: Mix ¼ C. taco seasoning, ½ C. lime juice, and a handful of chopped fresh cilantro. Pour the mixture evenly over 2 lbs. boneless, skinless chicken thighs and chill ½ hour. Grill over medium-low heat until done; shred and serve. *Serves 8*

Whip up a variety of taco meats *(try **Ooo's & Ahh's Tacos** and **Run-for-the-Border Chicken** on the facing page as well as **Steak Street Tacos** on page 60)* and dump into separate bowls *(we used foil loaf pans set into a 9 x 13" dish)*. Set the table with tons of toppings and let everybody build their own taco favorites. Serve up some **Citrus Blast Margaritas** for fun *(recipe on page 15)*.

START HERE FOR INSPIRATION

the Foundation

Flour tortillas	Taco salad shells	Tortilla chips
Crisp taco shells	Corn chips	

Tantalizing Toppers

Black beans	Lettuce	Cheese sauce
Black olives	Cabbage	Avocado Pico de Gallo *(page 61)*
Corn kernels	Green onions	Salsa
Jalapeños	Cheese	Taco Sauce
Tomatoes	Sour cream	

Fantastic Finishers

Lime vinaigrette *(for fish tacos)*	Malt vinegar *(for fish tacos)*	Lime wedges
		Fresh cilantro

Serves 4

A yummy and easy way to impress your friends, each and every time you make these.

CITRUS-SALMON SKEWERS

3 lemons, divided

2 T. chopped fresh parsley

3 cloves garlic, minced

1½ tsp. Dijon mustard

½ tsp. salt

⅛ tsp. black pepper

2 T. canola oil, plus more for brushing

1 to 1½ lbs. salmon fillets, cut into 1" pieces

Grease the grill grate and preheat the grill on medium-low heat. Juice one of the lemons and pour the juice into a bowl. Stir in the parsley, garlic, mustard, salt, pepper, and 2 T. oil; set aside.

Thinly slice the remaining two lemons. Slide the salmon pieces and lemon slices alternately onto four sets of side-by-side skewers (fold the lemon slices in half). Brush both sides with the mustard mixture.

Set a piece of foil on the grill grates and brush with oil; arrange the skewers on the foil and cook until the salmon is done, turning once.

Citrus Blast Margaritas

Cut 3 limes, 3 lemons, and 2 oranges in half; dip the cut sides in sugar. Set cut side down on a hot grill pan until lightly charred. Juice the grilled fruit into a pitcher, add any accumulated juice from the pan, and stir in 8 oz. tequila and 6 oz. simple syrup (or to taste); chill. Pour drinks into ice-filled glasses rimmed with sugar; add fresh fruit slices if you'd like. Tipsy fun around the grill!
Makes about 3 cups

Save Your Fingers

*When skewers get hot, fingers get burned. Always, **always** use tongs or oven mitts for flipping. Problem solved. And your fingers? They stay snap-happy.*

Serves a crowd

If you're cooking away from home, mix the dough ahead of time and tote it in the cooler. (Don't eat all the dough on the way though!)

CAST IRON COOKIE

Preheat the grill on low heat. In a big bowl, mix 1 C. softened butter, 1 C. brown sugar, and 1 C. sugar until light and fluffy; beat in 2 eggs and 1 T. vanilla. Slowly add 3 C. flour, ¾ tsp. baking soda, 1 tsp. sea salt, and ½ C. quick oats, mixing until blended. Stir in 1½ C. baking chips *(we used a combination of semi-sweet chocolate chunks, semi-sweet mini chips, and white chips)*.

Grease a 12" cast iron skillet with shortening and press the dough into it. Set on the grill, close the lid, and cook until golden brown and done in the middle, rotating the pan occasionally *(this could take 25 minutes or longer, depending on the heat of your grill – don't rush it)*. Cool slightly before cutting.

Serves 6

Chopping veggies not your thing? Pick up the pre-chopped variety at the grocery store. No excuses – you'll want to make these!

QUICK GRILLED VEGGIES

Preheat the grill on medium heat. Prepare fresh veggies by slicing into evenly sized pieces as needed *(we chopped up 16 C. of veggies, using a combination of red, green, yellow, and orange bell peppers, red onion, broccoli, mushrooms, zucchini, and cherry tomatoes – no need to chop these babies)*. Toss them into a big bowl and add ½ C. vegetable oil, 3 T. minced garlic, and salt, black pepper, and red pepper flakes to taste. Stir it all together, and dump onto a big grill pan, and set on the grill.

Close the grill lid and cook 10 to 15 minutes or until the veggies are crisp-tender and just starting to brown on the edges, stirring occasionally for even cooking.

Makes 6 huge burgers

Mouthwatering aroma. Mammoth size. Praise and adoration when the first bite is taken. Yup, it'll happen.

SMOKED DEEP-DISH BURGERS

Wood chips for smoking

1 T. butter

1 (8 oz.) pkg. sliced white mushrooms

1 red bell pepper, diced

½ C. chopped sweet onion

2 T. steak sauce *(use your fave)*

4 thick-cut bacon strips, cooked crisp & crumbled

3½ lbs. ground beef

1 beer or soda can for forming patties

12 thick-cut bacon strips, optional

Coarse salt & black pepper

12 slices of your favorite cheese *(we used sharp cheddar & Pepper Jack)*

Soak a great big handful of wood chips in water for 30 minutes, then drain. In the meantime, melt the butter in a skillet and sauté the mushrooms, bell pepper, and onion until softened. Stir in the steak sauce and cooked bacon and set aside. Line a rimmed baking sheet with foil and spritz with cooking spray. Form the ground beef into six equal-sized balls and arrange them on the baking sheet.

Clean the outside of the beer or soda can and coat it with cooking spray. Press the can firmly into a meatball to form a cup, pressing the edges of the meat to an even thickness and fixing any cracks; wrap each with two bacon strips, if you'd like, and secure with toothpicks. Remove the can and repeat with the remaining meatballs. Season with salt and black pepper and fill with the mushroom mixture.

Grease the grill grate and preheat the grill to 300° for indirect cooking. For a charcoal grill, toss a big handful of soaked wood chips directly on hot coals. For a gas grill, place wood chips in a smoker box. *(No smoker box? See DIY Smoker Pouch, below.)* Wait until the wood smokes for 10 minutes before grilling food.

Set the stuffed burgers on the cool side of the grill. Close the grill lid and cook 30 to 45 minutes; top each burger with two cheese slices. Cover and cook 1 to 1½ hours longer until the internal temperature of the meat reaches 160°, maintaining the grill temperature throughout. Do not flip the burgers. *A•MAZ•ING!*

DIY Smoker Pouch

Dump soaked wood chips onto a piece of heavy-duty foil. Fold over the edges of the foil several times to make a pouch, sealing the chips inside. Poke some holes in the top of the pouch and set it on the grill grate, directly over the burner on the hot side of the grill.

HOT DANG BUFFALO CHICKEN
WITH BLUE CHEESE SLAW

1 C. packed coleslaw mix

1 finely chopped Granny Smith apple

2 finely chopped celery ribs

3 T. crumbled Gorgonzola cheese

¼ C. chopped fresh parsley

1 finely chopped green onion

3 T. olive oil

1½ T. apple cider vinegar

½ tsp. sugar

Salt & black pepper to taste

1 C. wing sauce

½ C. unsalted butter, melted

⅓ C. ketchup

6 boneless, skinless chicken breast halves

Softened butter

6 hefty buns, split *(we used pretzel rolls)*

Ranch dressing

For the slaw, combine coleslaw mix, apple, celery, cheese, parsley, and green onion. Stir together oil, vinegar, sugar, salt, and black pepper; add to the slaw, stir to blend, and chill until serving time.

In a big zippered plastic bag, mix the wing sauce, melted butter, and ketchup; remove ½ cup and set aside. Add the chicken to the bag and toss to coat. Marinate at least 30 minutes.

Grease the grill grate and preheat the grill on medium heat. Toss the chicken on the grill *(discard the marinade left in the bag)* and cook until the internal temperature reaches 165°, turning to brown both sides.

Spread softened butter on the cut sides of the buns and grill until lightly toasted. Set the chicken on the buns; drizzle with ranch dressing and load on the slaw.

The simple ingredients in this marinade combine to create a flavor-packed sandwich. The addition of the ranch dressing and Blue Cheese Slaw? Unforgettable!

Makes 20

Use less seasoning for a toned-down version or add more for a fully cranked-up atomic experience. How much can your taste buds handle?

ATOMIC POPPERS

Preheat the grill on medium-low heat. Slice 10 jalapeños in half lengthwise; remove and discard the seeds and membranes. *(You know the drill: Always be careful prepping jalapeños – these beasts can do a number on your skin and eyes.)*

Mix an 8 oz. tub of cream cheese spread with 1 C. finely shredded Monterey Jack cheese, 1 tsp. chipotle powder, and 2 finely chopped green onions; stuff into the pepper halves. Nestle a mini smoked sausage into the filling of each and wrap a cooked bacon strip around the whole thing. Secure with toothpicks and set 'em on the grill; close the lid and cook several minutes, until the peppers are slightly tender and lightly charred and the filling is piping hot. *Yowza!*

Serves 4-6

These are so insanely delicious, they'll disappear fast! Luckily they're easy to throw together, so you can make more. Hooray!

GARLIC & ONION CHEESY FRIES

Chop and cook ½ lb. bacon, reserving 1 T. grease from the pan. In the meantime, preheat the grill on medium heat.

Dump a 2 lb. bag of frozen crinkle-cut fries into a greased 9 x 13" foil pan. Sprinkle evenly with 12 oz. shredded sharp cheddar cheese. Top with 4 oz. cream cheese *(cubed)*, 4 sliced green onions, and the cooked bacon. In a bowl, stir together the reserved bacon grease, 2 T. olive oil, 2 large cloves garlic *(finely chopped)*, ½ tsp. red pepper flakes, and salt and black pepper to taste; drizzle evenly over the fries. Cover with greased foil and set on the grill about 30 minutes or until everything is sizzling hot, the fries are tender, and the cheese is melted. *Grab some forks and dig in!*

Serves 4-5

Easily double or triple this recipe to make as much as you need. These are super simple to put together and take only minutes on the grill.

ISLAND QUICK SHRIMP

3 to 4 T. orange marmalade

½ C. pineapple juice

½ C. coconut milk*

2 to 3 tsp. soy sauce

Coarse black pepper

1 lb. extra large shrimp *(about 20)*, peeled & deveined

Fresh pineapple, peeled & cut into 1" chunks

* The leftover milk can be frozen in ice cube trays and used in smoothies or other recipes.

In a big bowl, stir together the marmalade, pineapple juice, coconut milk, soy sauce, and a healthy shake of black pepper. Toss in the shrimp and set aside.

Grease the grill grate and preheat the grill on medium-low heat.

Push the shrimp and pineapple chunks alternately onto skewers and hit 'em again with black pepper. Grill a few minutes on each side or until the shrimp are cooked through and everything has nice grill marks, brushing with marinade while cooking.

Tropical Party Punch

Ahead of time, chill a 1.75 L bottle of coconut rum, a 1 L bottle of Blue Curacao, 64 oz. of pineapple juice (or more to taste), and 8 oz. sweet & sour mix. Pour everything together into a 6-qt. drink dispenser and fill with ice. Everybody needs a little "Vitamin C" now and then, right? Drink up! **Makes about 20 Cups**

For the Best Skewers

- *Pair foods the same size and with the same cooking times if you're putting them together on a skewer.*

- *Cut food into 1" or 1½" cubes; any smaller and they'll fall through the grate.*

- *Eliminate flaming bamboo skewers by wrapping foil around the portion without food or simply laying that portion over a piece of foil.*

A potato bar is a fun and easy way to feed a bunch of people. Our recipes each serve about eight, but make what you need for your group.

POTATO BAR

Grill-Baked: Poke holes in 8 baking potatoes; wrap in foil. Cook over indirect heat 45 minutes, until tender. *Makes 8*

Slices: Cut 5 lbs. of potatoes into ½"-thick slices; put into a bowl with 1 C. chopped onions, ¼ C. chopped shallots, 3 T. olive oil, 2 T. seasoned salt, 1 tsp. garlic salt, and some black pepper. Dump into a greased 9 x 13" foil pan, cover with foil, and set over direct low heat for 30 minutes, until tender. *Serves 8*

Tots: Put a big handful of thawed tots on eight squares of greased foil; season to taste. Fold foil around tots and heat over direct low heat 15 minutes. *Serves 8*

SET IT UP

Load the grill with potatoes *(try the recipes on the facing page and **Garlic & Onion Cheesy Fries** on page 23)*. While the potatoes cook, set the table with plates, silverware, napkins, and glasses. Put your favorite wines on ice. Place toppings in bowls. Add the potatoes to the table when they're cooked. Finish the night with a no-fuss dessert, like *Boozy Banana Boats* on page 9.

START HERE FOR INSPIRATION

the Basics

Butter	Sour cream	Shredded cheese

Tantalizing Toppers

Cooked bacon, ham & turkey

Pepperoni slices

Veggies like broccoli & asparagus

Grilled corn kernels

Green onions

Tomatoes

Mushrooms

Guacamole

Cheese sauce

Chili

Gravy

Pesto

Salsa

Fantastic Finishers

Fresh basil, cilantro, dill & chives

Seasoned salt, garlic salt & onion salt

Crushed red pepper

Makes 6

The quintessential grilled cheese sandwich meets boisterous beer in this true grilled version of the classic.

BEER-CHEESEWICHES

Preheat the grill on low heat. Stir together 3 C. shredded sharp cheddar cheese, 1 C. shredded Swiss cheese, 1 T. Worcestershire sauce, 1 tsp. dry mustard, ¼ tsp. cayenne pepper, and ¼ tsp. salt. Slowly stir in about ½ (12 oz.) bottle of Pilsner, until the cheese is just barely moistened.

Divide the cheese mixture among 6 slices of Texas toast; spread evenly but not all the way to the edges. Put another slice of bread over the cheese and squish together. Spread a little melted butter over both sides of the sandwiches and arrange on the grill. Close the lid, but don't walk away. In just a couple of minutes, peak at the bottom. When you see golden brown, flip and repeat. Enjoy immediately, but watch out for the molten cheese flow.

Makes 18

The perfect size for stuffing, these little portabellini mushrooms make an ideal appetizer. Go on – grab one!

CREAMY SPINACH-STUFFED MUSHROOMS

Preheat the grill on medium heat. Remove the stems and gills from 18 portabellini mushrooms and rub melted butter over the outside of each.

Stir together 1 (8 oz.) pkg. softened cream cheese, 2 C. shredded sharp cheddar cheese, 2½ tsp. minced garlic, and 4 C. firmly packed chopped fresh spinach. Stuff the cheese mixture evenly into the mushrooms and season with salt and black pepper to taste. Set them on the grill, close the lid, and cook about 10 minutes, until the 'shrooms are cooked and the filling is hot and melty. *Oh yeah, that's the stuff!*

Serves 12

Beer-infused onions. Juicy brats. Sweet & tangy kraut. Winning combination. Simply one of the best ways to serve brats to a crowd.

BEER TUB BRATS

3 (12 oz.) cans beer *(your favorite kind)*

2 yellow onions, sliced

2 tsp. minced garlic

¼ C. butter, cut up

12 brats

12 brat buns

Make-Ahead Kraut *(recipe on facing page)*

Set a 9 x 13" foil pan on the grill and add the beer, onions, garlic, and butter. Preheat the grill on medium heat and let the onions cook at least 15 minutes.

Toss the brats on the grill grate alongside the pan and heat until they're thoroughly cooked and browned. Put the cooked brats into the beer mixture to keep warm and moist until serving.

To make it easy for serving, set everything by the grill; put the brats on buns and pile on those beer-infused onions and a load of kraut. *That's right, a load of kraut.*

Make-Ahead Kraut

In a big bowl, mix 2 (32 oz.) jars sauerkraut (drained), 4 celery ribs (sliced), 1 each red and green bell pepper (diced), and ½ yellow onion (diced). Whisk together 2 C. sugar, 2 C. distilled white vinegar, ½ C. vegetable oil, and ½ tsp. salt and stir into the veggies. Cover and chill 24 hours to let those amazing flavors blend. Everybody needs a good kraut recipe, and this is it! **Makes about 10 cups**

Brats 101

• *Brats can be purchased precooked or uncooked.*

• *For precooked, simply toss 'em on a hot grill until warm all the way through and lightly crisped on the outside.*

• *For the uncooked kind, grill over medium-low heat 15 to 20 minutes, to 145°. Or precook in liquid and then toss 'em on the grill until browned.*

Serves 4

This pizza crust is quick and easy and needs only 20 minutes of resting time, giving you... 20 minutes of resting time.

CHICKEN ALFREDO PIZZAS

2 C. bread flour

1½ tsp. sugar

1 (.25 oz.) pkg. active dry yeast

¾ tsp. salt

¾ C. warm water *(110°)*

Olive oil

½ (14.5 oz.) jar Alfredo sauce *(we used roasted garlic parmesan)*

2 Roma tomatoes, finely diced

1 green bell pepper, finely diced

½ small onion, finely diced

6 oz. chicken breast, grilled*

1 C. finely shredded mozzarella cheese

½ C. baby spinach, chopped

Grated Parmesan cheese

Coarse black pepper

Stir together the flour, sugar, yeast, and salt in the bowl of a stand mixer. Using a dough hook with the mixer running, add the water and 1 tablespoon plus 1 teaspoon oil, and beat until the dough forms a ball. Continue to beat for 5 minutes, until the dough is nice and smooth; transfer to an oiled bowl, cover with plastic wrap, and let rest for 20 minutes. You can use the dough now or chill up to 24 hours *(then let warm to room temperature before rolling out).*

Preheat the grill on low heat. Flatten the dough into a large rectangle on a floured flat cookie sheet, then transfer to a well-greased grill pan, patting to fit. Score with a knife into four rectangles. Cook until the bottom is nicely browned and the dough is firm enough to flip. Remove the pan from the grill, cut dough on the score lines, and flip the dough over.

Brush the edges of the crusts with oil. Spread sauce to within ½" of the edges. Divide the tomatoes, bell pepper, onion, chicken, mozzarella, and spinach among the crusts and sprinkle liberally with Parmesan and black pepper.

Return the pan to the grill, close the lid, and heat until the dough is cooked, the cheese is melted, and everything is nice and warm. ***So good!***

* Or use 1 (6 oz.) pkg. grilled chicken like Carving Board brand.

Servings vary

These are great to make up ahead of time, and then just warm 'em up on the grill. A little fanciness wrapped in foil.

HAM & SWISS CROISSANTS

For each sandwich, split a croissant in half horizontally and spread some cherry preserves on the cut sides. Pile on sliced deli ham and add slices of Swiss and Gruyère cheeses. Put the top of the croissant over the cheese and bundle it up in foil.

Place on a warm grill for 10 to 15 minutes or until heated through. ***Easy-peasy and super yummy.***

Serves a crowd

Any dip is a go-to staple for a crowd, but THIS dip – with lots of smoky BBQ flavor – will be an instant hit!

BBQ CHICKEN SKILLET DIP

Preheat the grill on medium-low heat. Cut 2 (8 oz.) blocks of cream cheese in half horizontally and set the pieces side by side in a greased 12" cast iron skillet. Dump 1 (15 oz.) can each corn and black beans *(drained & rinsed)* and 2 sliced green onions on the cream cheese. Mix 1 C. sour cream, ½ C. BBQ sauce, 1 tsp. garlic powder, 6 oz. grilled chicken breast *(or use a 6 oz. pkg. of grilled chicken, like Carving Board brand)*, and ½ C. each shredded Pepper Jack and cheddar cheeses; dump over the veggies in the pan and top with a little more cheese. Set the skillet on the grill, close the lid, and heat 10 to 15 minutes or until the cheese melts and everything is warm. Toss on some chopped red onion and diced avocado and add a drizzle of BBQ sauce. Serve warm with tortilla chips. **Dig in people!**

DILL-ICIOUS RYE PULL-APART

1 (1 lb.) round loaf
   rye bread

8 oz. shredded dill
   Havarti cheese

½ lb. dried beef *(a.k.a.
   smoked beef)*, chopped

½ C. unsalted butter,
   melted

1 to 2 T. dry ranch
   dressing mix

Dill weed to taste

Preheat the grill on medium-low heat for indirect cooking. Cut the bread from the top down in ¾"-wide lengthwise and crosswise slices, without cutting through the bottom; set on a large sheet of heavy-duty foil and roll the foil up around the sides of the bread, creating a nest to hold the bread in place.

Set aside ¼ of the cheese and push the remainder into the cuts of the bread along with all the beef. Stir together the butter and ranch dressing mix and drizzle evenly over the top. Sprinkle the set-aside cheese and the dill weed over all. Cover with a piece of foil and place the loaf on the cool side of the grill. Close the lid and cook 12 to 15 minutes, rotating once or twice.

Remove the top piece of foil, close the lid again, and cook 12 to 15 minutes longer, rotating occasionally. ***Ooey, gooey, cheesy dill-iciousness!***

This eye-popping pull-apart loaf is so incredible, you'll be making it again, and again, and again...

Makes 8

Giardiniera – a combo of pickled veggies – adds color and crunch to these juicy burgers. Find jars of it in your grocer's condiment aisle.

ZESTY ITALIAN BURGERS

- 2 lbs. ground beef
- 1 (3 oz.) pkg. prosciutto, chopped
- 1 (16 oz.) jar Chicago-style Italian giardiniera, well drained & coarsely chopped, divided
- 1½ T. Italian seasoning

- Softened butter
- 8 ciabatta rolls
- Garlic pepper
- 8 slices provolone cheese
- Pickled banana peppers, drained & sliced
- Arugula

Grease the grill grate and get the grill good and hot.

In a big bowl, mix the ground beef, prosciutto, ⅔ cup giardiniera, and Italian seasoning *(just use your hands to make it easy).* Shape the mixture into eight patties and press a dimple into the center of each.

Turn the grill heat down to medium. Arrange the patties on the hot grill, close the lid, and cook several minutes on each side, until done to your liking.

Meanwhile, butter the cut sides of the rolls and sprinkle with garlic pepper; toast lightly.

Add a cheese slice to each burger and let it melt. Plop these juicy burgers on the toasted rolls and pile on banana peppers, more of the giardiniera, and some arugula. ***Delizioso!***

Fast Fresh Bruschetta

Cut 2 pints of cherry tomatoes (about 48) into pieces and mix with 2 T. olive oil, 12 sliced fresh basil leaves, and a hefty dose of coarse salt and black pepper; set aside. Cut a loaf of Italian bread in half lengthwise, drizzle with olive oil, and toast lightly on the grill. Remove from the grill and get some garlic on there (garlic powder or a swipe from a cut garlic clove). Pile on the tomato mixture, slice the bread, and enjoy. **Serves 12-16**

Head to the game and load up the grill with all the brats and dogs your gang can eat. Keep the rest simple and enjoy the festivities.

TAILGATING – BRATS & DOGS

Sweet Touchdown Kraut: Mix 1⅓ C. chopped green bell pepper, 1 C. chopped onion, 6 T. brown sugar, 4 tsp. yellow mustard, 2 tsp. caraway seed, and 3 C. drained sauerkraut. Dump onto foil and create a sealed pack, then heat on the grill. *Makes 5½ cups*

Try these winning ideas

Pack lots of brats, dogs, and buns in your cooler. *(Check out the recipes for **Beer Tub Brats** on page 30 and **Spiral Fun Dogs** on page 7.)*

Toss in some chips and a simple side dish *(the kraut recipe above or **Make-Ahead Kraut** on page 31 are fan favorites).*

Bring a few roasting sticks and toast 'mallows to perfection over your dying coals. S'mores anyone?

Whip up a big-batch cocktail in a drink dispenser and tote it in an ice-filled cooler to share with all your game-day buddies *(**Spiked Iced Tea** on page 47 is a perfect choice)*.

Don't forget napkins, plates, and plastic utensils. And remember to bring cups and ice, too.

Put an assortment of condiments into small mason jars; add lids and stack in the cooler. Use permanent markers to label a wide craft stick spreader for each. *Score!*

START HERE FOR INSPIRATION

the Basics

Ketchup   Mustard   Pickle relish
Kraut   *(several kinds)*   *(sweet & dill)*

Tantalizing Toppers

BBQ sauce   Roasted red   Pineapple
Chutney   peppers   French fried
Chili   Onions   onions
Pork & beans   Avocado   Crushed potato
                                  chips

Servings vary

Make everything ahead of time, then just toss the cornbread on the grill when you're ready to eat.

HOT HONEY CORNBREAD SLABS

Make an 8.5 oz. pkg. of corn muffin mix according to package directions and bake in an 8 x 8" pan *(or whip up a batch using your favorite recipe)*. Let cool, then cut into squares *(if more than ¾" thick, slice in half horizontally, too)*. Beat together ½ C. softened butter, 1 finely diced jalapeño, and 2 T. honey.

Preheat the grill on medium-high heat. Coat the cornbread slices with cooking spray and set on the grill for a couple of minutes on each side, until crispy. Spread the butter mixture on the cornbread and serve immediately.

Serves a hungry crowd

This makes a great big heapin' pan of goodness! Serve it right from the grill or slide onto a cookie sheet to move.

SMOKIN' GRILLER BOURBON BEANS

Preheat a grill on low heat. Put 1 (11 x 15 x 3") foil pan inside another one and coat with cooking spray.

Drain 2 (3 lb. 5 oz.) cans pork and beans, 2 (15 oz.) cans black beans, 1 (15 oz.) can kidney beans, and 1 (15 oz.) can cannellini beans and dump into the pan. Add 1 (18 oz.) bottle BBQ sauce, 1 finely chopped jalapeño pepper, 1 chopped red onion, and 1 each chopped yellow and red bell pepper. Stir in 1 lb. chopped and cooked smoky bacon, up to 2 lbs. brown sugar *(go on – throw it in there)*, and 1 C. bourbon. Cover tightly with foil and place on the grill; close the grill lid and cook for ½ hour, until bubbly; remove the foil and cook ½ hour longer, until hot and awesome. *Oh yeah!*

Serves 4

Whip up a whole bunch of this seasoning blend to keep on hand. Use it on everything you grill, all season long.

JUICY STEAKS & MUSHROOM STIR-FRY

2 tsp. coarse salt

½ tsp. dried basil

½ tsp. black pepper

½ tsp. ground ginger

½ tsp. dried minced garlic

4 (8 oz.) steaks *(we used New York Strip)*

1 tsp. toasted sesame oil

2 T. peanut oil

8 oz. sliced fresh mushrooms *(any kind)*

2 cloves garlic, thinly sliced

1½ tsp. finely chopped gingerroot

¼ C. roasted red bell peppers

½ C. stir-fry sauce

¼ tsp. red pepper flakes

Fresh basil, optional

Grease the grill grate and preheat the grill on medium heat. Stir together the salt, basil, black pepper, ginger, and minced garlic for a simple but sensational seasoning blend.

Rub the seasoning mixture over both sides of the steaks. Grill the meat until it reaches the perfect doneness for you, flipping once *(see the chart below for some guidelines)*. Pull the steaks off the grill, tent with foil, and set aside.

Set a big sauté pan or wok on the grill to preheat a few minutes. Drizzle in the sesame and peanut oils. Add the mushrooms and cook a few minutes, until they're just becoming tender. Toss in the sliced garlic and gingerroot and cook for another minute or so. Add the roasted peppers, stir-fry sauce, and red pepper flakes.

Spoon the mushroom stir-fry over the top of the steaks and toss on some fresh basil for extra glam.

What's the Perfect Steak? You Decide.

RARE (125° with a cool red center)

MEDIUM-RARE (130° to 135° with a warm red center)

MEDIUM (140° to 145° with a rosy pink center)

MEDIUM-WELL (150° to 155° with a slight pink center)

WELL DONE (160° with a brown center)

Makes 12

The aroma of this chicken will draw a crowd – in a good way! The taste? You could say it's finger lickin' great!

SWEET SOUTHERN DRUMSTICKS

¼ C. brown sugar

2 tsp. minced garlic

4 tsp. salt

2 tsp. black pepper

12 chicken drumsticks

½ C. of your favorite sweet BBQ sauce

3 T. pure maple syrup

2 T. ketchup

In a zippered plastic bag, mash together the brown sugar, garlic, salt, and black pepper to form a paste. Toss in the drumsticks, seal the bag, and rub thoroughly until the chicken is coated. Chill overnight.

Grease the grill grate and preheat the grill on medium heat for indirect cooking. Whisk together the BBQ sauce, syrup, and ketchup and set aside.

Arrange the drumsticks on the hot side of the grill, cooking until browned on all sides. Then move them over to the cool side and cook 30 minutes longer, until the internal temperature of the chicken reaches 165°, basting with the sauce several times near the end of cooking.

Spiked Iced Tea

Mix the zest of 1 lemon with ¼ C. sugar; set aside. Cut the zested lemon in half and set one half aside. Squeeze the juice from the other half into a 3-qt. pitcher. Stir in 3½ C. prepared lemonade, 3½ C. sun tea or unsweetened iced tea, 1½ C. bourbon, and ¼ C. sugar; chill. Rub the rims of drinking glasses with the set-aside lemon half and dip rims into the sugar mixture. Fill with ice and pour in the tea mixture. Sippin' sensational! **Makes about 8½ cups**

Serves 8

Here's a recipe that you can really get excited about – keep it handy because you'll be making these a lot!

TURKEY-APPLE MEATBALLS

Grease the grill grate and preheat the grill on low heat. In a saucepan, whisk together 1 C. BBQ sauce, ½ C. grape jelly, 4 tsp. apple cider vinegar, and ½ C. chicken stock. Set the saucepan on the grill to slowly warm up.

Shred 2 unpeeled red apples onto heavy-duty paper towels and squeeze out the excess juice; dump the apples into a bowl. Add ½ lb. finely chopped, uncooked bacon, 2 lbs. ground turkey, and 1½ tsp. salt; mix with your hands until evenly combined. Use a 2" cookie scoop to form meatballs and thread onto side-by-side thick skewers. Grill 35 to 45 minutes, until cooked through, turning and drizzling with the warmed sauce occasionally. Serve the remaining sauce with the meatballs.

Makes 6

Nothin' says summer like fresh sweet corn! Support your local farmers' market and start grillin' now! You'll be glad you did.

WOW CORN!

Preheat the grill on medium heat. Remove the husk and silk from 6 ears of sweet corn. Lightly grease the ears with olive oil and set directly on the hot grate. Grill for 15 minutes or until the kernels are tender and a deep golden color with some charred spots, turning often.

Take the corn off the grill; spread with mayo, sprinkle with chili powder, cotija cheese, and lime zest, and drizzle with lime juice. Toss on fresh cilantro for added color and flavor if you'd like. Serve it hot. ***Wow!***

QUICK BACON-AVOCADO PIZZAS

4 artisan thin flatbread pizza crusts *(we used Flatout Spicy Italian for addictingly intense heat)*

Olive oil

½ C. tomato sauce

1½ C. each shredded cheddar and provolone cheeses

6 bacon strips, cooked & chopped

1 or 2 Roma tomatoes, very thinly sliced

Red onion, finely chopped

2 avocados, seeded, peeled & diced

Make sure all your toppings are ready and setting by the grill, then preheat the grill on low heat.

Drizzle the crusts with oil and set them oil-side down on the grill for a couple of minutes, until grill marks appear. Flip them over onto a flat cookie sheet and spread each with about 2 tablespoons of the sauce. Divide half the cheese among the crusts. Top each with the bacon, tomato, onion, and avocado, and sprinkle the remaining cheese over all.

Slide the pizzas onto the grill and cook several minutes, until the cheese is melted and grill marks appear on the bottom. Serve hot.

There's a ton of flavor in each crisp bite. And your guests will still be raving long after they've eaten the last morsel.

Serves 4

This version of the Cuban sandwich is sure to become a much-loved, oft'-requested favorite. Easy to make for a bigger crowd, too.

ULTIMATE GRILLED CUBAN LOAF

⅓ C. melted butter

1 (1 lb.) loaf Italian bread, halved lengthwise

8 salami slices

8 tomato slices

Sliced onions

8 to 10 kosher baby dill pickles, halved lengthwise

About 5 oz. each sliced Gruyère, fontina, and American cheeses

Preheat the grill on low heat. Brush butter over cut side of each bread half and set them on the grill, cut side down. Heat until light golden brown. Remove from the grill and flip them over onto a big piece of foil.

To the bottom bread half, add layers of salami, tomato, onion, pickles, and all three cheeses. Plop the top bread half on the sandwich and wrap the foil tightly around it to hold all those layers in place, leaving the ends open.

Return the loaf to the grill and set a heavy pan on top; heat about 8 minutes on each side, until the cheese is melted and gooey.

Take that baby off the grill, slice it up, and snarf it down.

Simple Summer Beer

Pour 4 cans of your favorite light beer into a big pitcher. Add 1 (12 oz.) can frozen limeade, lemonade, or pink lemonade concentrate (thawed); fill the now-empty can with vodka and pour it into the pitcher. Mix it up real nice-like and pour into ice-filled glasses. Plunk in some lime slices (or lemon slices if you're using lemonade) and call it a day.
Makes 9 cups

Bring back the art of picnicing using some of these great ideas. Fire up the grill and get ready for some old-fashioned fun.

PICNIC BURGER BASH

Chive Butter Burgers: Mix ½ C. softened butter, 3 T. chopped chives, and ½ tsp. minced garlic; roll into a log and chill. Form ten thin patties from 1½ lbs. ground chuck. Slice the chilled butter and divide among half the patties; top with the remaining patties, sealing in the butter. Season with salt and black pepper. Grill over medium heat until done to your liking. Top with your favorite cheese. *Makes 5*

Black Pepper Mayo: Mix ½ C. mayonnaise with 1 tsp. freshly ground black pepper and 1 tsp. lemon juice.

Honey Mustard Mayo: Mix ½ C. mayonnaise with 1 T. lime juice, 1 T. honey and 1 T. Dijon mustard.

Grill up a plateful of juicy burgers *(Chive Butter Burgers on the facing page and Zesty Italian Burgers on page 38 are both great choices)*, find a shady spot on the grass, and spread out a tablecloth or blanket. Pack side dishes in resealable containers, fill squeeze bottles with condiments, and set out toppings. Pull out your favorite beverages, have a seat, and enjoy the great outdoors.

START HERE FOR INSPIRATION

the Basics

Ketchup & mustard

Pickles & relish *(sweet & dill)*

BBQ sauce & steak sauce

Lettuce, tomatoes & onions

Mayo *(try the flavored recipes on the facing page)*

Bacon

Cheese slices *(American, cheddar, Pepper Jack, Brie, or Havarti)*

Tantalizing Toppers

Salsa

Pesto

Chili sauce

Hot & mild peppers

Spinach

Caramelized Onions

Other cheeses *(try blue or feta crumbles, fresh mozzarella or goat cheese)*

Canadian bacon slices

Crispy shoestring potato sticks

Fried eggs

Makes 16

A swipe of cream cheese on pound cake. Pineapple, brown sugar, cinnamon, caramel, and pecans. Is your mouth watering yet?

CARAMEL PINEAPPLE POUND CAKE

Mix 8 oz. softened cream cheese, 3 T. brown sugar, and ⅛ tsp. cinnamon; set aside. Line the grill grate with foil, spritz with cooking spray, and preheat the grill on low heat. Core a fresh pineapple and cut into ½"-thick rings; sprinkle both sides with brown sugar and cinnamon and arrange rings on the foil. Cut 16 *(1" thick)* slices of pound cake *(we used plain and pumpkin-flavored)* and set on the foil. Heat everything until grill marks appear on both sides, flipping once.

Remove from the grill and spread the set-aside cream cheese mixture over the cake slices. Add a pineapple ring *(cut in half if needed)*, caramel ice cream topping, and toasted chopped pecans. ***Scrumptious!***

Serves 4

This is an easy side dish that goes with just about anything you're serving, and it turns out perfect every time.

ALMOST STIR-FRY RICE

Preheat the grill on medium heat. In a greased 9" round foil pan, stir together 1⅓ C. uncooked instant rice, ⅓ C. sliced fresh mushrooms, ¼ C. chopped green bell pepper, ¼ C. chopped onion, ½ C. chicken stock, ⅓ C. ketchup, ½ C. water, and salt and black pepper to taste. Dot with 1 T. butter. Cover with greased foil and seal the edges tightly.

Set the pan on the grill and heat for 12 to 15 minutes or until the liquid is absorbed and the rice is tender. Be careful when lifting that foil cover – the steam inside will be wicked-hot.

Serves 8

Since it's slow-cooked, this recipe is perfect for hangin' out by the grill with a cool beverage, enjoying the weather, and visiting with friends.

GRILL-SMOKED PORK LOIN

½ C. mild-flavored molasses

6 T. C. apple cider vinegar, divided

¼ C. Dijon mustard

¼ C. stone-ground mustard

2 to 2½ lbs. pork tenderloin

Salt & black pepper to taste

Mix the molasses, 4 tablespoons of the vinegar, and both mustards in a gallon-size zippered plastic bag. Add the tenderloin, zip closed, turn to coat the meat, and chill 4 hours. *(You've got plenty of time to toss around some bean bags before you start grilling.)*

Grease the grill grate and preheat the grill to 250° for indirect cooking. For a charcoal grill, toss a big handful of soaked wood chips directly on hot coals. For a gas grill, place wood chips in a smoker box. *(For **DIY Smoker Pouch** directions, see page 19.)* Wait until the wood smokes for 10 minutes before grilling food.

Remove the meat from the bag and reserve the marinade. Sprinkle the meat with salt and pepper; set on the cool side of the grill and close the lid. Cook 1 to 1¼ hours or until the internal temperature of the meat reaches 145°, checking a couple of times during cooking. *(Each time the lid opens, the temperature drops, so try not to check too often. Patience...)*

Pour the reserved marinade into a saucepan; add the remaining 2 tablespoons vinegar, bring to a boil on the grill, and cook until slightly thickened. Cut the meat and serve with the heated sauce. **Holy smokes, this is good!**

Leftover Pork? Try these ideas:

- *Slice and pack inside a crusty roll with BBQ sauce, slaw, & Monterey Jack cheese.*

- *Thinly slice and serve on crackers with a smear of mustard & pickled onions.*

- *Add chunks to a salad of romaine lettuce, apples & almonds; drizzle with mustard vinaigrette.*

Makes 8

Street tacos are small-ish, making them easier to eat and giving you reason to have multiples. Perfect for outdoor entertaining.

STEAK STREET TACOS

- 2 tsp. minced garlic
- 1 jalapeño, finely chopped
- A handful of fresh cilantro, chopped
- Juice of 2 limes
- Juice of 1 orange
- 2 T. distilled white vinegar
- ½ C. olive oil
- Coarse salt & black pepper to taste
- 2 lbs. steak *(we used Top of Iowa Sirloin)*
- 8 small flour or corn tortillas
- Cooking spray
- Avocado Pico de Gallo *(recipe on facing page)*
- Toppings of your choice

Mix the garlic, jalapeño, cilantro, lime juice, orange juice, vinegar, oil, salt, and black pepper in a big zippered plastic bag; add the steak, zip closed, and chill for a few hours.

Grease the grill grate and preheat the grill on low heat. Grill the steak until done to your liking, turning once. Take the meat off the grill *(but don't turn off the heat)* and let it stand 5 minutes before slicing across the grain into bite-size pieces.

Coat one side of the tortillas with cooking spray and lay them on the grill for a minute or so until warm and pliable.

Load the tortillas with steak, Avocado Pico de Gallo, and any other taco fixings you like.

Avocado Pico de Gallo

Chop a pint of cherry tomatoes (about 24) and toss them into a bowl with ⅓ C. diced red onion, 3 T. chopped fresh cilantro, 2 T. lime juice, and 1 T. olive oil. Stir in 1 peeled and diced avocado and season with salt and black pepper. Serve with chips, over grilled meat, or on tacos. So colorful. So simple. So g-o-o-d!
Makes about 2½ cups

Serves 4

Fast, super juicy, flavor-packed, and fun to eat. These four things make for very happy friends.

PORK POPS & TOASTED MELON

In a big bowl, mix 1 tsp. minced garlic, a small handful of chopped cilantro, 1½ tsp. white pepper, ¼ C. fish sauce, 1 T. soy sauce, ½ C. cream of coconut, 1 T. vegetable oil, and 1 T. sugar. Cut 1 lb. pork tenderloin into long, thin strips; add to the bowl and set aside at least ½ hour.

Set a grill pan on the grill and preheat on medium heat. Weave the marinated pork strips onto skewers and grill 5 to 8 minutes or until cooked through, turning once. Push fresh cantaloupe and watermelon chunks on side-by-side skewers, brush with oil, and sprinkle with salt and white pepper; toss on the grill for a few minutes. Serve immediately.

Makes 8

Impress your friends with these cinn-fully delicious dessert donuts, piled high with whipped cream and fresh fruit.

EASY GRILLED DONUT SHORTCAKES

Line the grill grate with foil and spritz with cooking spray. Preheat the grill on low heat. In a bowl, stir together ¼ C. sugar and 1 T. cinnamon. In a separate bowl, mix ¼ C. melted butter with 2 T. brown sugar. Set both aside. Separate the biscuits from a 16 oz. tube of jumbo refrigerated buttermilk biscuits; push a hole through the center of each.

Arrange the biscuits on the foil. Close the grill lid and cook 4 to 5 minutes on each side, until browned on the outside and cooked through. Remove the biscuits from the grill; one at a time, dip both sides in the butter mixture and toss around in the cinnamon-sugar to coat. Top with spray whipped cream and pile on the fresh fruit. *Yowza!*

INDEX